A WALL OF TWO

THE S. MARK TAPER FOUNDATION

IMPRINT IN JEWISH STUDIES

BY THIS ENDOWMENT

THE S. MARK TAPER FOUNDATION SUPPORTS

THE APPRECIATION AND UNDERSTANDING

OF THE RICHNESS AND DIVERSITY OF

JEWISH LIFE AND CULTURE

The publisher gratefully acknowledges the generous contribution to this book provided by the Jewish Studies Endowment Fund of the University of California Press Foundation, which is supported by a major gift from the S. Mark Taper Foundation.

A WALL OF TWO

Poems of Resistance and Suffering
from Kraków to Buchenwald and Beyond

HENIA KARMEL

AND ILONA KARMEL

Introduction and Adaptations by Fanny Howe

Translated from the Polish
by Arie A. Galles and Warren Niesłuchowski

UNIVERSITY OF CALIFORNIA PRESS
BERKELEY   LOS ANGELES   LONDON

University of California Press, one of the most distinguished university presses in the United States, enriches lives around the world by advancing scholarship in the humanities, social sciences, and natural sciences. Its activities are supported by the UC Press Foundation and by philanthropic contributions from individuals and institutions. For more information, visit www.ucpress.edu.

University of California Press
Berkeley and Los Angeles, California

University of California Press, Ltd.
London, England

For acknowledgments of permissions, please see page 119.

Library of Congress Cataloging-in-Publication Data

Karmel-Wolfe, Henia.
    [Poems. English. Selections]
    A wall of two : poems of resistance and suffering from Kaków to Buchenwald and beyond / Henia Karmel and Ilona Karmel ; introduction and adaptations by Fanny Howe ; translated from the Polish by Arie Galles and Warren Niesluchowski.
        p.   cm.
    Includes bibliographical references.
    ISBN 978-0-520-25135-9 (cloth : alk. paper)
    ISBN 978-0-520-25136-6 (pbk. : alk. paper)
    1. Karmel-Wolfe, Henia—Translations into English.   2. Karmel, Ilona, 1925- —Transla-tions into English.   3. Holocaust, Jewish (1939-1945)—Poetry.   I. Howe, Fanny.
II. Galles, Arie Alexander, 1944-   III. Niesluchowski, Warren.   IV. Karmel, Ilona,
1925- Poems. English. Selections.   V. Title.
PG7158.K286A2   2007
891.8'517—dc22   2007015644

Manufactured in Canada

16   15   14   13   12   11   10   09   08   07
10   9   8   7   6   5   4   3   2   1

The paper used in this publication meets the minimum requirements of ANSI/NISO Z39.48-1992 (R 1997) (*Permanence of Paper*).

Throughout the entire world, Rachel cries over her children, but they are not to be found. On the Hudson, the Thames, the Euphrates, Nile, Ganges, and the Jordan we blunder about in our confusion crying aloud: "Vistula! Vistula! Vistula! Our birth mother. Gray Vistula, river pink not from the rays of dawn, but rather from blood!"

JULIAN TUWIM

Contents

Illustrations

Preface

To an Unknown Reader

It is difficult today from the perspective of two years to contemplate the genesis of these poems.

We look at them in astonishment, powerless before their strangeness. It's as if we were meeting old friends after years of separation. They are known but foreign because of an impassible chasm—time and distance. Words spat out in a fever, screamed poems, now sound like weak whispers, almost inaudible. Experiences that we tried to reproduce in all their horrible reality have slipped into pallid outlines, already almost erased.

When we look at them right in front of us, the images come again: inscriptions upon the walls of prisons and camps, scrawled

---

From the collection *Spiew Za Drutami* (Song behind barbed wire), published in 1947 in tiny limited editions by the Association of Friends of *Our Tribune,* a Polish Jewish daily newspaper.

at the last moment by people who had already died. Cries for help, calls for revenge, a sentence terminated at midpoint, maybe only a name and a date, the terror of those days marked clumsily by a weakening hand upon a hard indifferent wall. Today only half-readable traces remain.

These poems are exactly that: inscriptions on a prison wall. They are feeble efforts to preserve a record. Why make such an effort to leave behind a trace and to transmit one's experience before it is all over? What forced us to do this? Was it the pain or was it a protest against the absolute end of things?

No. Having been taught by machine guns to think in categories of thousands and millions, we had reconciled ourselves to the unimportance of the individual. Did we write in order to transmit information and thereby incite people to later vengeance? No. In those days we understood the complete futility of trying to match any punishment to this crime.

And yet we did write for people in the future as an act of self-defense. We wanted others to discover in our suffering a meaning and a purpose: to ensure that millions did not die in vain as long as our experience was used as a warning for future generations.

These poems, and thousands of other creations, form one cry only: "Remember."

Henia Karmel and Ilona Karmel
Stockholm, April 1947
Translated by Arie A. Galles

Acknowledgments

Many thanks to Leon Wolfe, Joy Wolfe Ensor, John Wolfe, and Sarah Ensor for their support, their knowledge, and their time over the past seven years. Many thanks to Paulina Ambrozy, Krystyna Zamorska, Bob Perelman, Honor Moore, Margo Lockwood, Cris Mattison, and Xandra Bingley for their suggestions and support. Special thanks to Warren Niesłuchowski for his translations, for his work transcribing the Polish poems, for his advice and his insights into Polish history; and to Arie A. Galles for his commitment to these translations. To the editors of *Conjunctions, Zoland Poetry,* and *The Literary Review* who published some of these poems, my gratitude on behalf of the Karmel sisters; and to several unknown readers who corrected me. To the John Simon Guggenheim Foundation for support in 2005 and 2006, many, many thanks. For their close readings of every word and page—Rachel Berchten and Claudia Smelser—I am forever grateful.

Fanny Howe

Introduction

FANNY HOWE

The poems in this volume were written by a young woman who married at twenty, on the verge of incarceration, and by her sister, who was seventeen when they entered the Nazis' forced labor camps in 1943. The poems were written behind barbed wire in Poland and Germany by the two, who stayed together throughout the Second World War and who miraculously survived, as did their poems. The poems are rough, immediate, emotionally young, and determined by an early education in rhymed verse. The two sisters often used traditional forms that helped them preserve a learned and beloved culture in the midst of its destruction. And while these forms had already been abandoned by many modernist poets in Eastern Europe, they served a purpose for these two precocious prisoners. The poems express what it's like to dwell at the center of an anti-miracle. They were produced in that stretch of time in the twentieth century when something that couldn't happen did.

Henia and Ilona Karmel were born into an affluent and distinguished family in Kraków. The Karmel family was in the metal business, but there were many scholars, poets, and rabbis in their background who gave intellectual stature to their name in the Polish city. The sisters' parents, Mita and Hirsch, were more assimilated into the surrounding culture than the generation before, and the two girls were given a top education in standard government schools as well as a Hebrew gymnasium. The school system was so bicultural a student might never have to ask, "Am I Polish or Jewish?" Their days were passed on streets teeming with churches and Catholic liturgy and the chiming of bells on the hour and images of Christ and crucifix.

In their youth Henia was elegant and dark-haired, Ilona smaller and fairer. Both were well-loved and had a strong sense of their own value. They spoke Polish, Yiddish, and German. They read Hebrew and Western classics as well as Adam Mickiewicz and contemporary Polish poets. In 1939, when Henia was eighteen and had just graduated from school, she met a young man named Leon Wolfe in Zakopane, a resort town in the Tatra mountains that attracted artists and writers. It was a brief but significant meeting; then the war broke out.

"Let me try to sketch for you the Polish Jews as I knew them in my youth," Ilona wrote for a talk years later:

A heterogeneous world of city dwellers who lived in a complex and tragic contact with the non-Jewish community. Yet, be it because Polish society would not accept them; be it because they would not have felt at home in it, they remained intensely Jewish; seeing their hope in Zionism and, out of a kind of visceral loyalty, observing the Jewish customs . . . Then came the war. And even the assimilants, those believers in the ultimate acceptance of Jews by the Gentile world, had no illusion about the forces that barred the way to acceptance. "Poland without Jews"—this was the atmosphere of the thirties. The first evils of the Nazi occupation; the armbands with a Star of David, the closing of Jewish schools and stores were therefore painful yet not shocking. . . . It was the continuation of a familiar trend rather than a new development.

In 1940 there were 68,000 Jews living in Kraków, and many immediately fled to Russia and elsewhere. The Karmels set out to find relatives on the southeastern border of Poland. There the Russians tried to persuade them to cross over to safety, but Mita, of Russian heritage herself, refused, saying that she would rather be killed by the Germans than saved by the Russians. Although Russia had occupied and divided Poland several times dating back to 1750, the family would have been safer there. Mita's decision would prove to be a fatal mistake.

Disheartened and unable to find their relatives, the family returned to German-occupied Kraków, where a series of regulations limited the rights of Jews. All Jewish enterprises had to be marked by a Star of David, and the Municipal Registration Offices registered the entire Jewish population on forms marked with a yellow band. The Karmels managed to avoid being registered and found menial work. In 1941 special yellow identity cards were issued to Jews and the Karmels still spoke of escape.

Henia and Leon Wolfe met again; he took her to a café, where he had the embarrassing experience of having forgotten his money. A friend generously loaned him some. When he went to pay him back, Leon learned that the friend had been taken off by the Gestapo and executed. This marked the beginning of the approaching horror for him.

Leon wanted to leave Kraków when the ghetto was established in 1941, and Henia persuaded her parents and Ilona, then fifteen, to follow him to Brzesko, a little village outside Kraków. They all settled there and Henia and Leon were married in a traditional folk ceremony in June 1941, Henia wearing a wedding dress bought with money sent by a relative in the United States. But too soon trouble began again, and declared Jews had to leave the village, a scene described in one of Henia's short stories, published right after the war in the original Polish in the émigré magazine *Kultura* under the title "Wysiedlenie Widziane Oczyma Dziecka" (Deportation seen through the eyes of a child) and later published in English in *The Reporter* as "The Last Day" and reprinted in *The Best American Short Stories, 1962.*

The wagon bounces on the uneven road and splashes mud around. It is getting colder and colder: it drizzles. Mama wraps Pim in a blanket; he dozes off. He feels Mama kissing him, at first quietly and gently, and then harder and harder. He wakes up crying. He feels they are not the usual kisses. "Mama," he cries, "why do you kiss so hard? It hurts."

The wagon shakes over the muddy road. It is getting darker and colder and the drizzle changes to rain. In the distance, dark against the overcast sky, rise the church steeples of Izbica.

"Where are we going, Mama?" Pim asks.

Mama looks at him and doesn't answer right away. And then she says slowly, "To the trains. Just to the trains. . . ."

For a brief time they lived in the woods. Leon had secured an Aryan passport and Henia had dyed her hair blond, but people nonetheless kept asking him why he was with a Jewish woman.

The five moved on to Siedlicka, where some cousins owned a farm. It was during this sojourn that they were arrested, along with some Polish peasants, and were accused of aiding and abetting the partisans (who might be Polish, pro-Communist, or Soviet, pro-Poland) who had formed settlements in the nearby forests. They were held overnight in a barn and forced to dig their own graves. It was only when a cousin in the *Judenrat*—the council of Jews assigned to every community and beholden to the German government—saved them that they had to make immediate and potentially fatal decisions. Hirsch hesitated and told his wife, Leon, and his daughters to go on ahead without him; hurriedly they said goodbye and returned to the Kraków ghetto to find work. They never saw him again, and all were haunted by guilt at having left him. Ilona especially blamed herself for this event throughout her life, measuring all her subsequent actions against the moment when she impatiently hurried her family away from him. Once when her nephew asked her how, since she was so young at the time, she could have possibly decided to stay behind, she replied tersely, "Many did." All they learned later was that Hirsch had been taken to Treblinka.

Mita accompanied her daughters throughout the war, devoting herself to them. Until then she had had the life of many a sheltered European woman, not very happy in her marriage and irritated by money worries. But during the war she distinguished herself by her care for typhus patients and her supervision of her daughters in that work. She insisted that they remain strong and dignified, "because one day the world will be the world again." She was remembered long after the war for her acts of life-saving care, as were Henia and Ilona.

In Kraków Leon and the two sisters and their mother found

work at a paper company, where they recycled envelopes for the Germans. Ilona joined a Jewish resistance movement and was given a good measure of power because of her intelligence and energy. They were all Zionists at that time, devoted to providing mutual help to others escaping persecution and to retaliating against the enemy whenever possible. But there were many resistance groups whose actions overlapped with theirs: Communists, collaborators with the Allies, Russians, Poles, not all of whom were adult men. Young people like fifteen-year-old Ilona were frequently used as message bearers and information gatherers, but Ilona emerged as a teen leader, even giving orders to one of her teachers. The general principles that bound these groups were economic and social. Zionists, with the founding of the kibbutz movement in 1937, believed in national ownership of land and capital worldwide and settlement in parts of Palestine with the active participation of the Arab people. This was their Zionism then.

Throughout 1942 conditions in the ghetto grew more desperate, with deportations and murders emptying the population day by day. Those who remained worked as slave laborers while the Germans constructed concentration and labor camps in nearby rural areas. Plaszow, where the Karmels and Leon would be sent, was built on two Jewish cemeteries. From February 1943 until September 1944, the camp was commanded by the notorious Amon Goeth.

It was a bright sunny day in March 1943 when Henia, Leon, and Ilona sat at the ghetto gate waiting for the call to march to the Plaszow camp. Leon took off his coat with his Jewish badge on it and an officer grabbed him and threatened to beat him. Henia snatched the man's hand, saying "Don't hurt my husband," while a crowd of fellow deportees watched in horror. It was Kommandant Goeth himself who from then on hovered threateningly around Henia during inspection. Under constant threat of separation, Henia and Leon promised each other that they would return to Kraków when the war was over and find each other there, no matter what.

In the camp Leon had the job of breaking apart consecrated headstones, one of which bore the name of a childhood friend of his. Tractors moved across the available soil, unearthing decomposed bodies wrapped in prayer shawls. For a time Ilona worked as a cleaning woman to a German family in Kraków and smuggled food back to the camp to share with others. Henia worked in an ammunition factory for eight to twelve hours a day, without food or the milk that would have reduced the effects of the toxins on the workers' bloodstream.

While in Plaszow Ilona heard a story that had a deep effect on her. Years later she wrote it down for her family this way:

> I will speak of one known to me not by his name but by his deed—a rabbi chosen to die in a "selection" of old people conducted on the orders of camp commandant Amon Goeth by members of the Jewish camp police. When they reached the site of execution—the top of a steep hill—the policeman charged with carrying out the order begged the rabbi's forgiveness. He granted it. He then asked for a moment's time. They agreed. The rabbi turned, looked toward the camp—a place where despair turned to sordid vice—reached out his hand in blessing, and said the prayer, "How good are your tents, O Jacob, your tabernacle, O Israel."

As he spoke, the rabbi was looking at a camp where there were two hundred barracks and other buildings crammed together. Up to fifty thousand people passed through the camp, a tenth of whom were murdered there. Barbed wire, watchtowers, endless construction, and pits where their bodies were dumped. Gypsies and Communists who resisted the Nazis were buried there. Poles, Frenchmen and Frenchwomen and Germans and Jews and young Hungarians were transported there and there was a latrine planted on top of the mass grave in the quarantine area. The blessing continued: "Thanks to Your abundant kindness, O Lord, I am able to enter Your house."

Later in 1943 the Karmel sisters and their mother were sent on to the forced labor camp at Skarzysko-Kamienna in central Poland. Again they were put to work in a HASAG plant where they faced monotonous machine work, typhus, hunger, and overcrowding.[1] The camp was divided into three *Werke,* or sections. The Karmels wound up in Werk C, the worst. Here prisoners were turned into objects if they did anything out of place—they were painted different colors and wrapped in paper sacks and displayed as walking skeletons to strike horror into the hearts of other prisoners.

The first two sections were primarily devoted to manufacturing ammunition and the third, Werk C, to the production of underwater mines filled with picric acid. Working twelve-hour

---

1. HASAG was an acronym for Hugo Schneider Aktiengesellschaft, the third largest private German company (after I. G. Farben and the Hermann-Göring-Werke) to employ forced labor during the war. The existing factories at Skarzysko-Kamienna produced ammunition during Poland's independence and were immediately useful to the Nazis. HASAG was put in charge of the factories in 1940 and began using Jewish forced labor there in 1942.

shifts under horrific conditions, prisoners turned yellow and died from exposure to the acid. Selections in which any prisoner might be shot by factory police occurred randomly. Jewish prisoners had to haul the bodies of other prisoners to a mass grave. Only when there began to be a critical shortage of factory workers did conditions improve at all.

One barrack was called the Rabiner Barak because Rabbi Yitzhak Finkler led his Hasidic followers in prayer and study there. There were Hungarians and French resistance workers in the Skarzysko-Kamienna camp. Inside the barbed wires there was continual resistance and it was here that many of the poems in this book were written. A non-Jewish worker in the plant gave Henia and Ilona extra worksheets to write on. Using the blank side of the worksheets, the sisters composed their poems in pencil (also very difficult to get hold of) and then concealed them. There was an invention of cultural life at this camp, really a form of reminiscence that included prayer, drawing, song, poetry—all with references and sources instantly recognizable to those present.

Felicja Karay has described the ways music and literature were written in the Skarzysko-Kamienna forced labor camp, where she too was a prisoner:

> The social and cultural life evolved in two stages. The prisoners first gave expression to the cultural and intellectual values on which they had been raised at home and in school. But mere nostalgia could not fulfill the prisoners' cultural needs for very long. The appalling conditions and contact with the autochthonous population of the camp and its many masters gave rise to frustrations and fears that demanded a different outlet. Thus the second stage began—coping with the new reality by means of

original creations. Nearly from the start, the cultural life of the camp was of two forms: relating to the past or to the present. This dichotomy was typical of all four types of cultural activity: religious life, community singing, original compositions and spontaneous or organized shows.[2]

Passover was an especially difficult time—potatoes and beets were used for the haroset and grain coffee substituted for wine. The seder text "How is this night different from all other nights?" made everyone weep. (Years later Henia's story "Passover in a Concentration Camp" would become part of the liturgy in many synagogues.) Sometimes a choir sang Yiddish and Hebrew songs, including the camp song "O'er the Cannons" and "Horat ha'Galil," to which people danced the hora. Overhead were heard the screams of sirens and the thudding of Russian weapons. The Karmel sisters recited their own poetry and then concealed it inside their clothing.

Sometimes gifted Jewish prisoners had to perform for the German administration and police. Some of the police granted these prisoners special favors. One notorious commander of Werk C, a woman of great power referred to as Katerina the Second, protected artists and encouraged performance in her sphere, while allowing hundreds of others to die of starvation.

In the summer of 1944 the Germans began to retreat and mass killings took place. Six hundred ailing prisoners were murdered

---

2. Felicja Karay, "Teaching the Holocaust through Music and Camps Literature Written in the Camps," paper presented at the International School for Holocaust Studies, Jerusalem, October 13, 1999, pp. 2–3 (see http://www1.yadvashem.org/download/education/conf/Karay.pdf).

in the camp; 250 prisoners escaped from Werk C into the forest, and almost all of them were killed by the Germans, Ukrainians, or local Poles. The Karmel sisters and their mother were part of a mass selection of six thousand prisoners sent on to a HASAG plant outside of Poland, to one of the multiple forced-labor camps attached to Buchenwald, which sits only six miles from the robust city of Weimar. High on a hill, shadowed with black and bony trees and with a view to distant mountains, the camp was in full view of passing farmers and children until April 1945. Buchenwald was originally intended for political opponents of the Nazi regime, Polish Catholics, separatists, Roma and Sinti, members of the French resistance, homosexuals, Jehovah's Witnesses, and Jews. Misfits, they were all called as they were put to work in the armament industry.

In a section of HASAG-Buchenwald set aside for women, Henia and Ilona still had the poems with them, sewn into the hems of their dresses. Long afterwards survivors would remember the two sisters reciting them, Henia's voice being particularly memorable for its musical quality.

How these poems came to be read again, outside the camp and the war, is a story in itself. It began with the April 1945 evacuation of HASAG-Buchenwald, when the SS sent prisoners on forced death marches. Nearly 28,000 prisoners were forced by the Germans to walk in circles along the roads and through the forests outside the camp. In this process, many of them were deliberately crushed by Germans in tanks and shoved into a pile. Henia and Ilona and her mother were three of these. They were pushed into a field of corpses and abandoned. Shortly thereafter another group of prisoners passed by, one of whom was a cousin of the Karmels. In the chaos Henia was able to tear open her clothes and hand her cousin all of the poems. She repeated her husband's name to her cousin and begged her to get the poems to him in Kraków if he was still alive.

The next day—the last day of the war—a Polish woman who had been working as a slave laborer on a nearby farm came upon the heaps of corpses and by chance saw that some people were alive. She summoned her boss, who came to see for himself. This was how Henia, Ilona, Mita, and a Hungarian woman came to be driven by horse and cart to a nearby hospital, where there was only one doctor left. They had been mutilated by the tanks, this trip was agony, and their bodies would never be whole again.

In the hospital the sisters each had a leg amputated.

Their mother, Mita, died there.

The sisters were moved to another hospital, where the nurses either intentionally or thoughtlessly increased their thirst with salty food. Here they at least had a radio and were able to learn a few things from the news. Henia had no idea whether Leon was still alive. Eventually they were taken to Leipzig. For six months they lay in a hospital there, knowing nothing of the outside world. Their poems had long since disappeared.

After the war Leon returned directly to Kraków to look for Henia and Ilona as promised. The surviving Jewish community had established a relocation and reunification center there, where Leon met other prisoners from the HASAG plant. They told him that Henia, Ilona, and their mother had been killed in an "accident" during the camp's evacuation. He nevertheless remained unwilling to believe the worst. When the sisters' cousin managed to locate him and give him the poems, Leon asked whether Henia and Ilona were alive when she saw them. She told him they were, but that they could not have survived, given their terrible injuries. Once he heard that the cousin had seen them alive, Leon began a wider search. His friends thought he was crazy to hope. He became reclusive on the one hand and continued his search on the other. Carrying the poems with him, he went to outlying towns and as far as Breslau, three hundred miles to the northwest, in search of the sisters.

One night in an industrial center for textiles, he met some Russians who asked him to cooperate with them in securing the plants in the area from German partisans, who were still hiding in the mountains. That night they stayed with their guns among Persian carpets, pianos, and long curtains in a magnificent villa. He couldn't sleep because it was so comfortable and instead lay on the floor. One of his companions found some alcohol that they all drank, and Leon made them listen while he gave the first reading of the Karmel sisters' poems in the postwar world.

Leon then went to work in a plastics factory privately owned by a German refugee. He learned of a memorial service being planned for the two girls by family and friends in Kraków. Heartsick, he agreed to let it happen. The service took place in a large cinema. On September 28, 1945, two days after the melancholy event, a man in Leipzig heard about it. Realizing that the service was for the Karmel sisters, he went directly to the Jewish Historical Commission and notified them of the sisters' whereabouts. The commission sent a telegram to Leon informing him that Ilona and Henia were in St. Elizabeth's Hospital in Leipzig. Leon wanted to rush there at once but his friends persuaded him to write a request on stationery, in Russian and Polish, asking his boss if he could go to Leipzig to buy dyes for the factory.

There was still an ugly postwar atmosphere of revenge and

The telegram sent September 29, 1945, announcing that the Karmel
sisters are alive in a hospital in Leipzig.

suspicion hanging over Poland and Germany, but Leon got per-
mission to travel, and in a car patched together from other car
parts, he drove the five hundred kilometers from Kraków to Leip-
zig. A distinguished Russian friend came with him. Beside him
he carried cigarettes, vodka, and ham to bribe Russian border
guards along the way. Many hours later Leon and the Russian
entered a huge hospital complex in Leipzig. Leon asked the first
nun he saw if she knew the Karmel girls. "You are the husband!"
she cried and took him to Henia and Ilona's room.

Their reunion was overwhelming to all three. But almost
immediately Leon and his friend had to return to work in Kraków.

Miraculously, the car made it home to their door, when it basically fell apart in one puff. Leon at once began to seek better medical and reconstructive care for the two sisters. On his way to a prosthetics factory one day he happened to meet a Swedish naval officer who was with the International Red Cross, and he explained the sisters' situation to him. The officer asked Leon if he had relatives in America who would take responsibility for them later, after the sisters were restored to health. He did. The officer was leaving for Stockholm but promised to contact Leon within two days. The man was as good as his word and called from the Swedish embassy in Warsaw with visas for Henia and Ilona. Both needed reconstructive surgery, and Sweden was known to offer the best rehabilitation treatment, so this encounter was yet another miracle. The two sisters were taken to Stockholm.

Soon Henia was walking with a prosthesis, but Ilona's injuries were so severe she stayed at the Karolinska Institute for two years. There, both of them began to develop an interest in narrative. Years later Ilona would write in her notes, "Each piece of writing is for me a laboratory in which an idea can be verified only in and through the lives of the characters. Any idea that fails to become concrete in them, or that forces even the least manipulation of the characters must be rejected. If, at the end, the characters choose a sacrificial death, it is I hope not because of an *a priori* scheme, but because the trials and errors of their inner growth make this choice inescapable."

In 1948 Henia and Leon moved to New York with their newborn son John. Ilona followed in 1949, having taken an English-language correspondence course from Oxford while she was hospitalized. She eventually found her way to Radcliffe College. While there she fell deeply in love with the philosopher and physicist Francis Zucker, and he with her, and they married soon after meeting. They moved to Germany for his career and there Ilona worked in an orphanage for many years while she wrote her masterpiece, *An Estate of Memory*. In 1978 she began to teach writing at MIT. Both sisters would write only prose fiction in English—possibly because English was exempt from the source of their experiences. Their fiction was, in that sense, already a translation of past into present, a rejection of the experiential taste of the mother tongue in favor of something strange but uncontaminated.

Henia wrote short stories over the years, and both sisters wrote two novels each, but the manuscript of poems remained in a drawer. Henia spoke often of the poems with pride, while Ilona brushed off her contribution as worthless. Henia always said that Ilona was a better novelist than she, and Ilona said her sister was a better poet than she. They were critical of each other's work over the years. But as Leon Wolfe remarked, "They were as one."

As for the publication history of the poems, Leon typed and sent them to relatives in the United States. In New York an ad hoc group called the Association of Friends of *Our Tribune* (*Our Tribune* having been the last Polish Jewish newspaper existing in Warsaw before the war) managed to publish them. It was 1947. The sisters, still hospitalized in Sweden, were asked to write a preface to this collection. This came as a complete surprise, since no one had asked their permission to print the poems, but they were happy to see it through. They never learned who read these poems or how they were received; the collection was titled *Spiew*

Za Drutami (Song behind barbed wire) and included the statement that prefaces this volume.

In 1999 a Hebrew edition of the poems was published. Felicja Karay, a campmate of the Karmels, enlisted the aid of Ruth Stern, who translated many of the 180 pages. Henia was no longer alive and Ilona wanted little to do with the poems by then, so Leon supervised this transaction. In the end Ilona was glad to have the poems published and was moved when the Kraków Society in Israel held a publication party in Tel Aviv. But again, she never learned how the poems were received. As it turns out, the Hebrew collection was made up of a selection almost identical to the poems chosen for this volume.

There are Karmel poems in Hebrew and Polish scattered around. In 1988 in the bookstore at Auschwitz Leon found anthologies of camp poetry, published in Poland, that included poems by the two sisters. Felicja Karay included some of their poems in her book *Grenades and Poems: The Work Camp at Hasag-Leipzig.* And they come up in the memories of survivors. As for the letter to Julian Tuwim at the end of this volume, it was never intended to be read by him and never was.[3] Henia wrote it as a pupil might convey a message to her teacher, without planning to mail it to him. After this the manuscript of poems lay in a drawer in New York until 2000, after Ilona died, when fam-

---

3. Julian Tuwim (1894–1953) was a major Polish poet who began the Skamander school of experimental poetry that broke away from the high rhetoric of earlier Polish poetry. He wrote about despair in modern urban life. His collection *Slowa we Krwi* (Words bathed in blood), published in 1926, would have been well known to the Karmel sisters if only because his poetry was recited aloud in the camps. In 1944 he published a manifesto, *My, Zydzy Polscy* (We Polish Jews), that lamented the war years.

ily members passed on the 180 pages to me as an old friend of hers. The entire manuscript of poems, in Polish, is in my archive at Stanford University's Special Collections.

It was Henia who once mailed her own poem "Christ Lonely" to the Roman Catholic pope Karol Wojtyla, because he came from Kraków and had played ball in the streets with her husband when they were children.

Key to Translators

AG   Arie A. Galles
WN   Warren Niesłuchowski

Handwritten manuscript of a poem written by Ilona.

THE POEMS

Autobiography

Childhood

This story begins like any other.
A childhood tale as ordinary
as milk and flowers. A world so small
it could be contained within four walls.

The story begins in an aura of tenderness
and calm though also in a world
so enormous that Mother's hands
had to protect us.

There was a children's room
with blue walls and ceilings
and when the day broke open
outside the window the sky
merged with our ceiling.

And everything then was golden blue.

That day—my God—was short.

We couldn't fathom all its wonders
before the light began to fade
and the sun disappeared. The lamp
flickered sleepily, darkness trailed
from its hiding places out in the town.
It glued itself to our windows—
it was stifling—and we tossed.

And then that darkness became something else.

Whispers, rustles, chatters
from a primeval woodland
joined the silver patterns on the wallpaper
and became forty thieves.

Bad dreams, black covers, light walls.
Unknown folk. Alarms.
Until a milk-like river of light
poured between you and that,
and you were safe enough to run
into your mother's arms . . .

There were stickers in a hundred colors,
butterflies, flowers slick as a rainbow,
and big bonbons with a surprise
inside their sweet chocolate shells.

The world was glutted with secrets.

Written into the blue walls were elves,
water nymphs, slender and skittish,
hampers, baskets, naughty gnomes,
and spirits that hid in the corners of the room.

Every day, my God, was too rich
to fathom. Brimming with miracles.

Mother's room, pale lilac, held
enchantments deep in large drawers
among ribbons, blouses and veils,
yellow lace (écru) scented

with the rolling press. Violets
decorated the broken fan,
and peacock feathers. Yes,
silk and taffeta and satin—

too lovely to be described! . . .

Number 16 Dluga Street is still there,
I am sure, crammed in
between the same houses
that were standing when I was a child.

In the park the maples bloom and droop.
But childhood is gone
fast and for good, who can say
where it went? The world around

shriveled up and grew small.
I don't know how. Now
nothing is mysterious.
Nothing survived the pogrom
and its time, not the elves,
sprites, gnomes, or little folk.
They were not saved
any more than the secrets in the drawers.

The fantasies fell slowly, heavily
and brutally.
The tub is no longer an ocean,
the whale nothing to fear
and the chestnut is just a chestnut.
What is good fortune, I ask . . .

Soon fear doesn't lurk in the dusk.
Darkness is tempting instead.
The dangerous unknown
looks good. A mother is superfluous.

Farewell, childhood! Hello, youth!

A splendid, gigantic
world of stories and adventures
awaited me at fourteen
when we still counted the years.

And before a new way of computing
time began—by days, hours, fears,
minutes, menace, ashes,
ruins, pain, despair, terror, suffering, murder.

Yes, that became the way
we measured time when I was fourteen.
There are no words to explain.
Only tears.

ILONA KARMEL
AG

The March of the Fifteen-Year-Old Boys

They were right in the middle
of a game of cops and robbers—
breathless from running
and drunk on the fun—
with schoolbook pages
rustling in their minds.
They were set to return to the quiet classroom
when they ran into the grip of history.

It lunged at them
and ordered them onto the field.

Left, right, left, right!
was its awful command.

The sun gleamed like a red cut
over the march of those children
and doom squirmed in front of the light
and wrapped itself around their feet.

Left, right!

Don't cry, my brothers. Sing.
Drown out your fears with music.
Bang trumpets and hammers.
We're all going together
down this terrible path.

"Why isn't anyone clapping?
Aren't we being brave hiding our grief?"

You know that you will never
hear your mother whisper "My son" again.
This is a road of no return.
See the angry sergeant, he's upset
because you can't bear your load.

The general, there, go ask him.
Maybe you'll learn something—
even how to dress ranks.

Left, right, left, right!

See the wind ruffle the flag.
Look, the last ray of sun is gone.

The wind is blowing wildly
around the commander in chief,
the field marshal himself and his adjutant.

They look straight ahead while it howls:
"Hail, Caesar, those who are about to die salute you!"

HENIA KARMEL
AG

Us

One, two, three, four . . .

Numbered and nameless

And clothed in standard-issue rags

Here they come—to prison

To be introduced

To trembling lamps,

Drizzle, rifles and hard rain,

To sufferings without number.

HENIA KARMEL
AG

Procession

Two marched by
in striped prison garb
then two more in rags.
After them came four
on stretchers.
Their bodies jerked up
comically at the night sky.
Half-naked with broken legs.
A frozen cadaver and then
just beside the prison gate
came four more stretchers.
One pressed a blood-soaked cloth
across his face.
The parade went on
while we watched in dread.
The rag man on the litter was dying.
And at the end, four from a nightmare
lugged on their heavy shoulders
a bundled body.
They couldn't cope and let it drop.
It screamed in its own blood.

HENIA KARMEL
AG

The Land of Germany

Wires, wires everywhere.

Barbed and bright

Like mad-dog teeth.

Like pots with their cracks stapled shut.

Like fear blockers.

Like Germany itself—

Fearful, fanged, easy to break.

HENIA KARMEL
WN

German Uniform Mania

Excuse me, sir, just a minute.
Could you kindly tell me
where I can find a human being?
That's right. A normal one
in a suit or something. Maybe
double- or single-breasted.
Black or navy, no brass buttons,
no uniforms. A person.
Are they out of stock?
Is this mania for uniforms all we get?
Is this today's fashion?
What a shame!
I thought maybe there would be one specimen left,
    perhaps in the zoo in Berlin.

HENIA KARMEL
WN

Pursuit at Night

All night the sirens howl like hyenas
and the way they go on
proves that the night is deaf.
Futile calls for help
are swallowed by the dark.

Now there's a bang and a flash
that seems to rush on a streak
the length and depth of the sky.

It penetrates the stars and clouds
like a hideous mole
that creeps, snoops, investigates,
eavesdrops, spies and zigzags.

"Where's my enemy?
Where's my enemy?
Here? Here? He's maybe here?"

You beast rabid from throat to snout.
Bite, bite into the mark. Your enemy is here.
Ready, aim, fire, maybe you'll hit your mark.

The clouds and stars seem to bleed
and to swim. Then a propeller emerges.
It's a bird and it's silver.
Can they catch it? Can they hit it with rifles?
Clatter, rattle,
its propellers shiver like laughter.

Like teeth grinding, like fangs chewing down,
it aims for the ground—
with a bang!—Bomb-spit is what earth gets.

HENIA KARMEL
AG

To a Friend from a Strange Planet

Once on a March day
you swam into the blue street,
your gaze fixed
on wind-driven clouds.
You crossed a field
warm from sunlight
inhaling the fresh grass
spread fallow before you.

My friend, my alien
from another world, do you
hear my voice? It was then
that the end of the world began
and infinity too.
There was no place
more horrible than the Jewish ghetto.

Now you gazed on the plume
of the sun's rays and your eyes
looked gentle and wise.
Yet you didn't know
that this was the day of destruction.
The last day.

The day of annihilation.
It began without Judgment.
Or the triumphal horn
of an archangel. Instead
asthmatic trumpets wheezed
shrill prophecies of Armageddon.

That was the biggest disappointment.
An absence of glory.
Just ugly bleats and whines
announcing the arrival
of a shiny limousine—doom.

White rifles, white sun.
Quiet streets and inert
crowds looking on and children
with ancient faces were helpless.
The first cadaver flopped in mud.
The first shots were muffled.

It was so quiet only the sobs
of mothers sounded,
stifled so no one could hear
and no child would ask,
"Mama, why is the milk so bitter?"
(The milk was bitter from cyanide.)

Then it wasn't quiet anymore.
A trumpet blasted horribly.
A shot rang out—a scream—
Friend, you heard that scream
and went on walking.

This was a famous day.
It became Everyday for Jews
but you didn't pause.
It was spring in the ghetto.

The executioner washed
his bloody palms and yawned.
That limousine sped by again.
There was no space on the ground
for graves. Children slept.
And God above was silent!

You who said nothing
while people were dying
pray for eternal life for them
if only in human memory.
It's not retribution we want
because how could it add up?

My friend from a strange planet
did you even understand
that my song was a scream?

ILONA KARMEL
AG

Fatherland

Please find me an ordinary place to live.
Forgotten, barren, a piece of ground.
Rocks, a desert, I don't mind
If it can be my homeland.

A simple fishing village.
Or something tucked inside a mountain.
Where nothing much grows and no one wants to go.
Its citizens common, quiet people

Unknown to the outside world.
If they accept me as their guest
And murmur, "Our house is your house always."
Then let this be my homeland.

But first let them forgive me for my mistake.
It has been a curse and a disgrace
To have dark eyes and speak a strange language.
To be a Jew.

But I will praise that country all my days.
I will be good to it and work
There among its rocks.
I will sing and my blood will warm such a place.

Oh faraway country, still a fantasy to me,
I will live for you and die on command
If you will first forgive me for my race
And let me call you home . . . wherever you are.

ILONA KARMEL
AG

The Day Will Come

German factories—one of these days—
will be engulfed by sirens—
that awful animal yell—and the workshops
will empty, machines go still
and hours will pass and no one will come.
Even the detonation plant will stop work.

Motors, engines, car parts, rubber tires
and all such utilitarian objects
owned by the German Reich! Yes,
all those factories will be empty at last.

The foreman will stare at Herr Direktor
who will spread his hands and say,
"But I don't understand . . ."

Herr Direktor, if you don't understand
why are you so nervous?
Why are you yelling that this is sabotage?
Why are you shaking with rage?
Sending the police out into the streets?
Can't you see, really, that liberation is coming?

The city has woken up from a long sleep
and is being rocked by the young
and their crazy chants. The city has got
back its sight. The streets will erupt at night
and spill a river of blood. Revenge!
For time lost! *Allons enfants de la patrie!*

HENIA KARMEL
AG

A Night among Frenchwomen

1

A melody, a minuet,
a crinoline dress.
Fire of revolution.
The Marseillaise.
And Madame
in the French section of the camp.

Please let me think about these, Madame,
and this way quiet myself.
I'm sure that our cruel life can be relieved
by a remembered fragrance of lilacs.

If only you could take me by your slender hand,
Madame, and lead me
through a reckless dance
in memory of July and the revolution.

The Bastille destroyed!

And other holy places that will revive me.
Because I'm still young.

Teach me, Madame, a song
as simple as the scales
to get my heart beating again.

Maybe then I will wake up
to the words *bientôt, bientôt.*

Let me sit beside you
and weep, Madame, in your arms.
It will be like sharing a holiday bread
when I can whisper
my sadness to you and remember
with you the colors of Paris and her wine
and pretend that life is worth living.

2

I don't know how it happened
but it was as if the walls dissolved
and we were in Paris again
in the Latin Quarter.
A melancholy tango echoing . . .
It smelled as it did years ago—
of jasmine and lilacs and the wind rustled
over shady parks, alleys, gardens
and our blood—French and passionate—
stirred between us.

3

Sisters of mine, listen to the rhythm
of that song calling us to dance.
Let's stamp and trample the ground
like people who are free from slavery,
who are outside of prison!
Paris is dancing.
Let's dance too.
Come on! They won't notice us

in the shadows, they will only guess
that we are lovers of life, that's all.
Nothing more or less.
We aren't guilty for having dark eyes
and curly hair. Or for being foreign.
Our happiness is the same as theirs
(except full of tears).

Paris, take us away!

4

Why are you sad, tiny Madlone?
Tiny, pale Madlone. Why tears?
Did a tango blow into your dreams?
Toulon remembered
in its sweetness makes you weep?

Oh Madlone, tiny, pale Madlone,
I hardly know you
but guess it must be good
to have a home in Toulon
where someone pines for you.

How could I know, Madlone,
tiny, pale Madlone
how great such sorrow is.
Homesickness and trust
in the existence of your beloved Toulon?

To have someone to miss,
like you do, Madlone,
so tiny and pale,
is surely awful. The white letter
brought your cries for Toulon.

This evening the mist
is heavy. It is fall
and on days like these
it is worse, still,
to have no letters at all.

Please smile for me, Madlone,
tiny, pale Madlone,
sister, though foreign,
remember at least that Toulon
is waiting for your return.

Nowhere for mine.

HENIA KARMEL
AG

The Mark on the Wall

Praxia Dymitruk, Praxia, Praxia
why did you write your name all over the walls?
Is this pain written down
or resistance to life's passing?

Were you, too, afraid to disappear?
Without a sound? No one to miss you
because you belonged to no one?
Is your name all you owned, Praxia?

I understand you, little Russian one.
Such a sweet stem of a name.
For a girl so familiar though never known.
Praxia Dymitruk, Praxia, Praxia.

HENIA KARMEL
WN

Snapshots

1

Curtain fell

Comedy over

Orchestra stopped

on the upbeat

Actor vanished
before the audience
even met him

The first act the last.

2

Hey take a look at this crematorium
It's brand new
You push a button
Electricity zooms through
the line and then the wheel turns
at a dizzying speed
Then it just stops. A shout
And it's done.

3

Hello! I'm a slut.
Don't believe it?
Honest to goodness.
My father was decent
but his daughter's a whore,
or if you prefer, a courtesan
properly raised
(though not pedigreed,
professionally speaking)
until I had to sell myself.
My name is Number 906.
And guess what? I still write verse.

4

And do you want to know
what I do for a living?
I'm not joking.
I sort shell casings
It's the best job
because killing is good
and time passes fast
when the work has a purpose.

5

What was that?
A tomato tossed
to us discreetly
with a laugh?

No, not at all.
It is a bloody scrap
of someone's heart
ripped apart

by pity.

HENIA KARMEL
AG

On Learning of the Latest Transport

That barrel pointed at our heads
won't point the other way.
The latest transport has been reported
by a symphony of gunfire.

The music is funereal, horrible.

Locked up in ghostly, dismal, secret cells,
wild, final, futile, treacherous,
still we the people
want to escape! To live!

We despaired when we heard
all that racket. Some of it was our hearts thumping.
This thumping even muted the volume
of the gunfire.

At the same time each heartbeat seemed pathetic
indicating a secret hope
beyond our terror.
Next thing, we heard sobbing.

HENIA KARMEL
AG

The Days of Vengeance

When the time for revenge comes
The heavens will recede and the sun
Will hide behind a screen of tears.

All the stars will react and tremble
And our despair, our hate
Will turn every beam of light into dread.

When the time for revenge comes
The planet will roll to a stop.
The ocean will hold its breath and pause.

The universe will contract silently
When the time for revenge arrives.
The only trumpet will be blown by the wind.

But we will be weighed down with so much pain
On that day, instead of blood
It will be our tears that fall, bitterly and long.

ILONA KARMEL
AG

Flight for Life

Flight from the toil
Of slave labor.
Sickness and hunger.
Flight from monotony.
Flight to life.
Flight is life.
Flight from blows,
Bullets, threats
And the fear of them.
Flight from the stalker
Who wants me to die.
Flight is life.
Flight is my life,
My hope, my dream.
I have no home.
I have no hope.
Flight from those
Who wonder:
Why bother?
Go where?
To whom?

For what?
No answer!
Flight for me is life:
My life with no controls.

ILONA KARMEL
WN

The Origin of a Poem

First there is a soul and a seed
Swelling, secret, deep.
A troubled premonition.
Dusk, germination.

The seed is sharp, patient.
It spreads into words,
Strophes, sound, branches.
Then you are its gardener.

Its rhythm comes like a gale
That sways in your soul.

Your pen is your shovel
Transplanting these words
Into ridges on paper where
They flower in air, tear off and disappear.

ILONA KARMEL
WN

Terrifying Laughter

When thinking puts the brain to sleep
In a spidery web, when memories sneer
And make fun, when evil is real and hope-killing
Then I laugh. Terrifyingly, I laugh!

When I feel crushed by a weight
That can't be lifted—and it never is—
When despair grows strong and sorrow drifts past
Then I laugh. Terrifyingly, I laugh!

When I see my youth expiring and time
Gnawing away at my best years,
And my freshness sickening and my thought
Becoming dumb, then I laugh, terrifyingly, I laugh!

And when I can't remember your hands
And the tone of your voice is lost
And I can't recall the way you looked
Then I want to laugh. But there's none of it left.

HENIA KARMEL
WN

Our Blood

Listen! That's our blood pulsing—
purple, wild, red—
foaming like the power of fire
that can't be contained.
Never!

When you remember how close we came
to fainting in the sun,
spellbound by a strange face,
how suddenly our blood surged up
and we struggled, madly?

Only twenty years old—remember!
It was then our blood began to sing
behind bars, wires, everywhere.

ILONA KARMEL
AG

Time

(To the new year, 1944–45)

We tried to overcome time.
Time. Inimical, cruel,
above all inscrutable.
Beyond and despite us.
Time the incomprehensible.
Like water eternally
flowing. Secretive,
evasive, fleet, impenetrable.

People tried to cut it up
on a calendar, into years,
days and quarters, to trammel
and control it. Time
the indomitable and terrible
other that won't give in
to human will. Our enemy.

It could be a cloud, a clap
of thunder, a thought, a fog,
a gale, a target, a dream.
Time drives forward cynically.
Beyond months, days, years.
It leaps out of the heavens,
deals in death and doesn't die.

HENIA KARMEL
WN

Strange Poem

This heart has been deaf and dumb
for a long time, but today, hit, it shouted
while the wound burned.

In one misunderstood word, the cut
opened up yet again but the throat
was struck mute at the larynx.

One small reckless word
can throw you down and take you back
while the world rolls on in evil clouds.

Oh of course nothing really changed.
It was just a heart reacting to life
for a minute, only to expire again.

HENIA KARMEL
WN

A Child's Vision of Peace

On a very nice day, out of the blue,
Grisha, Ivan, Hans and Johann
will notice that the sky is clear.
Hey, and the grass is lovely and smooth.
Wheat fields are both gold and green.
So then, they'll wonder, why ruin them?
They'll lean on their guns
and the sun will burn so bright
it will bring tears to their eyes.
Soon Vanya, Volodya, Ivan, Hans, Karl, Fritz
and Johann will spot each other
across that pretty view.
They will blush and laugh nervously.
Johann, over here, will sigh:
"My God, that guy with the red star
has childish blue eyes." And Ivan
will reply: "Wow, guess what?
That one in the green uniform
is dark-eyed and faithful as a dog."
All these eyes, gazing back and forth,
will lead to shouts and sobs:
"How did this happen to us?
Did it have to go this way?
Weren't we just obeying orders
every day? I don't get it.
But, hey, it's morning now.
We have to forget.
Never again! Don't look back!"

And in a child's vision, or a poem
they will cross the field cautiously,
watching out for bullets,
until Johann and Ivan
stand face to face.
Ivan will whisper "Z-drahst-vwy-tchee."
And Johann "Guten Tag."
They'll grasp hands and hang on
as if they held a hammer and sickle.
Then they will swing:
Take that, and that!

ILONA KARMEL
WN

My Life

My life consists of the banging
shock absorbers
and hydrosulfuric stench,
and the boiling, stinking, panting
factory line.

Day and night
lamplights
always flicker out there.

Every day! Fog and gloom.
The labor is stretched
to breaking, expectations
are extended.
Dreams go undreamed.

Cemetery days.
One after the other.
White caskets, the planks
of our bunks
await our thoughts
that grow ill in this hateful prison block.

HENIA KARMEL
AG

Verses

I bet you're thinking "Not more poetry!"
You might even add,
"Please, even if it's not bad."

But guess what? This isn't verse at all.
It's made with the ink of tears.

God has sent down a spell
and a wall and every word
inside is cursed.
This is not poetry. It's an alarm bell.

It's a scream, a thunderburst,
syllables in a rush.
The same old sounds
you always hear but now insane.

The universe is distressed
when no one knows how to say things fresh:

"Sorrow, reverie, lamentation, dream,
chaos, wilderness, ruined youth,
disease and desire
for help or revenge . . ."

That's the kind of poetry
that this is.

ILONA KARMEL
WN

An Answer

How can I act so calm?
Strangely on prison pallets you go quiet.

Then days are your sleep, sticky and dreamy.
At work you are of a piece with the machines.
A screw that turns one way only.

This kind of calm feels evil and weak.
I've lost any sense
of purpose or meaning.
I'm calm because I don't care anymore.
It doesn't bode well.

I have no belief and no desire,
no expectations.
I'm like a spectator
who is not present at her own life
but I know it's escaping me.

In the end, I'm just wiped out.
That's all. Don't worry. My calm comes
from being exhausted and forgotten.
It doesn't bode well.

HENIA KARMEL
AG

The Demand

I have something rude to say to you,
Life, Fate and World.
I don't want happiness or peace
the way hundreds of thousands do.

No, not while eternity burns inside of me
raw and violent with stars
and days bursting and re-creating
their rhythm that pounds in my own heart.

I feel it. I want it.
While I am young and passionate,
don't let my heart break!
Let it stay strong enough to carry me on.

I just want to wander
with my longing and my hurt too.
And even if I am slowed by pain
I still want to seek the truth!

ILONA KARMEL
WN

The Abscess

An abscess pulses.
Pus collects inside it.
Agony pumps in
the mouth. Repulsive.

My dreams are aching.
They pulse and hammer
and have an appetite.
Do you feel that knife?

It cuts to the bone.
It's a pen. Ready
for surgery. Slice!
Do what you can, words.

Burst the sorrow out.
Ah yes. Like that.

ILONA KARMEL
WN

To Our Professors

You taught us to strive
for perfection, to live up
to the words of prophets
and poets. To shun mediocrity.

You taught us to seek the truth
in certain ideas, taught us to love
the magic of language, to express
our awe at the universe.

You charmed us with stories
of heroes, history, myth,
until the holy revolution
(Equality, Fraternity)

danced before our eyes.
But with a certain word—*humanist*—
and another—*genius*—
you also ensured our suffering.

How? We had no defense
against the world in front of us.
You should have taught us
how to grab life by the throat,

to slam it between the eyes
until it staggered and fell—
to shout so we were heard,
to break down gates

and to get used to the sight of blood.
Professors, didn't you ever learn
that there is no place on earth
for humanists?

Why, why did you plant this dream in us?

H E N I A   K A R M E L
AG

Prison Nights

You'll never know how terrible
these nights have been.
Braided around hunger and brain
like a spiral screwdriver, this pain.

You jump, wild-eyed, from your stinking bunk
into the dark and onto the doorstep.

Outside fog shapes the windows into tombs.
You want to scratch and howl like a dog.

Do you hear that ticking?
It's the clock clicking on each minute.

The night bleeds, is sticky.
Dawn, distant. A blind, weak sleep.
Then day and starvation arrive again
until night thoughts screw in the pain.

HENIA KARMEL
AG

Harmonica

My youth came back to me in a dream.
I was wild, hot blooded, ready for anything.
It showed in my eyes.

Who knows how such a memory returns?

Spring and summer gone already, now autumn
in the real world. But what's that sound?

A harmonica—"Nagni, nagni li!"

In my dream my eyes seemed to shine
with enchantment during the dance.

Oh but I remember best the heat and the charm

of being swept up by a strong arm—
"Horat ha'Galil!"

HENIA KARMEL
AG

Fear in the Barracks

Near midnight fear enters the barracks.
Eyes shine wide from every plank
Exploring the blackened corners.
Soon dreams will be nightmares.

Near midnight in the barracks . . . fear.

    Rain often trails behind it
    Or moonlight finds a way in
    Or sometimes the wind groans
    Against the standing guillotine.

A blood-stained cloth whips there.

In the barracks around midnight . . . fear.

    Fear crawls up to the windows
    And sneaks around in shadows
    And sits on the bunks of those sleeping
    Freely providing images of horror.
    Like a hound it might howl at the door.

Around midnight fear circles the barracks.

The air is heavy, foul, still
Across the exhausted bodies.
Sleep is restless but breathless.
Someone springs up, another moans.
Someone gets scared and breaks into tears.

In the barracks close to midnight . . . fear.

Every night is a torment.
Stab after stab of dread
Gores each heart and finally cracks
The stone-cold sleep of some and they awake
Together to the horror: "Look there! The door!"

ILONA KARMEL
AG

When You Find Out

What will you do when you find out
that my young body was torn apart
by a bomb, shattered
into shreds and blood, beloved?
Well, don't weep then.

Or if you find out that typhus
ate me up and I struggled for life
on the ugly litters for the sick?
Beloved, please don't cry.

And when someone reports to you
in passing that I was starving
and poisoned from the bitter yellow picric acid?
No, don't cry, my only one.

But when you hear about my yearning,
my frenzy, my soul expiring,
pain and long nights of weeping,
mad days, mad days, tears, despair . . .

Yes, let your tears fall then.

HENIA KARMEL
WN

Encounter

When I stand before you on that long-awaited day,
you won't even know me.

"Truly you don't know me?"

You will stop and stare.

I will look at you through my tears until I hear you ask:
"My God, is that you?"

"Have I changed so much?"

"No, not really. It's just that I kept you alive in my dreams
and you had different eyes then. Transparent green like
    the sea.
Now they gaze on me so sadly, and are troubled by grief.
Before you had a lovely red mouth, childlike, joyful,
but it's all changed."

"Well then, look forever in wonder
at the sad and troubled eyes of your wife, now another."

HENIA KARMEL
WN

Two Machines

(For Basia Bogucka)

One machine turns and time rams down
while the gears bang and bang.

The other machine is a girl
with dark eyes and raked, scorched hands.

She grinds her time
over and over into the machine.

Her soul is gone and ghosts have moved in.
They ring and clang and laugh

and echo again and again.
Sometimes the silence gives her pain.

It's hard to haul emptiness around.
But those echoes won't let her alone.

ILONA KARMEL
AG

Christ Lonely

I was small, tired and bent, Christ,
when I went looking for you.
The world with its misty nights
and long lights had no end.

Through spring
and moody fall
I heard your name
being called from a chorus
of people and bells.

The cacophony hurt the air.
But I believed you were near
and my heart
beat with the gongs.

Honestly, I never really understood
the certainty behind
the claims made in your name.
I hung on though
and waited for you
until the day I faced it.
I would never find you.
How could I?
Painful truth:
You weren't even here.
You didn't exist any more.

So why did I keep on walking
(lost) over strange hard roads
only to find you
at last in an obscure place?

You stood alone at a crossroad.
And finally I saw you, and you cried.
You—more than a hundred times crucified.

HENIA KARMEL
WN

To the Rhythm of a Very Fast Waltz

In the weapons factory, the machinery
will sometimes waltz away the day.
(Once to the right and once to the left), it sways
so gracefully and seductively to the strains
of the dance that doom joins in with a "Bravo!"
and a wave. Here's a grenade!
Take this bomb. There's some gas.
Throw it and watch it blow up. Bravo
to the bang of that hand grenade!
All the apparatus and springs in the plant
move to one beat. Coquettish, you might say.
Sublime and courage-inducing machinery!

Then in the evening more music begins,
but this time a march with a one-two-three
the way nimble brown rats run up and down,
circling. And here on cue come the cops.
They don't even bother to ring a bell
or break down a door. They don't have to.
Please excuse us, they say, but is that a radio?
Surely you can't have ammunition here.
And in that corner? Allow us, sir.
Don't look so tragic, just lower your head.
I'm a good shot. It won't hurt.

And now a wild vision overwhelms them.
Without the waltz they can finally see
how everything is in reality.
Factories packed with bombs and grenades,
strange apparatus and automatic things.
They can see the hideous nature of this reality
and they'll scoot around, free of authority,
and clatter like sparrows in a tree
ahead of the marching of millions
screaming for revenge. Instead of a flag,
a bloody corpse will protrude from the throng.

ILONA KARMEL
AG

The Robots

Calling all parts! Calling all parts!
From the Oder to the Rhine, from Vienna to Berlin!
Today this is the big news:
something incredible has been invented.
It represents the apex of technology.
We will be announcing it over the radio
but also through megaphones and loudspeakers.
At last. Real live robots!

Read all about it!
Profit is guaranteed at one hundred percent.
Step up, sir, please take a look.
You might think it's a human being
but you're wrong because it demands nothing
and has no price.
It only works and works and works
and its labor is accurate and reliable
for fifteen, even twenty hours a day.
For a breadcrumb and a spoonful of food
it provides maximum speed, technology and skill.
No kidding. Please take a look, Herr Direktor.
It is intelligent, industrious, Herr Ingenieur.
Herr Wachführer, Herr Kommandant
what do you see? The golden age of industry
has come at last. Real live robots. Long live the robots!

What's that, sir? You're wondering if they break down?
Well, sometimes they do because of a little defect.
Say, a heart or a soul might react.
But it's nothing, sir. Don't panic.
Repairing the problem is incredibly simple.
You can just whack the robot on the snout
or whip it. Starve it even,
and it will rush right back to work
and make up for the time lost. No problem.
This is the truth, I tell you. We have made a perfect machine.

But wait. Of course a day will come when for no reason
the robots will stop and fall silent.
On that day some of them will howl, as if with great lust,
as if they feel life in them again, and they begin to listen.
Then unfortunately they'll weep from despair.
It's awful. They can't contain their misery.
They sound as if they're being flogged still, but this time
    by desire.
And at those times, these hot-blooded machines
go into the streets and gather and disrupt the peace.
They turn desperate, crazed by an unholy rage,
and move through the towns in a mass
spitting hate, mercilessly. Their dried-up lips crack open
and they all let out one furious cry:

WE WANT FREEDOM!

ILONA KARMEL
AG

Bread

I would love to have a loaf of bread.
Big, white and only for me.
The whole thing.
Fresh, hot and smelling of caraway seeds.
A crunchy crust
brown and crackling.

And to bite in with my teeth and chew
caressingly, blissfully, bite after bite,
against the roof of my mouth.
And finally to feel it heal and comfort
my empty stomach, my hunger that won't stop.

HENIA KARMEL
AG

Pears

A storm—a wind—the pears knocked down
onto the morning street. Now look—
broken-down women—locked in formation.

See how furtively they stop
to pick up the pears from the ground and eat.

Even their guard—a decent old man—
is ashamed to watch them guzzle and delight.

HENIA KARMEL
AG

Waiting

Although I waited for you every day
you didn't return.
No charming smile crossed the screen of memories.
Time, that comforter, had pulled you under its dark arm
and led you away into shadows
and the past. Now I don't know for sure
if any of it happened in my life
or if my heart, out of kindness,
dreamed up such happiness.

HENIA KARMEL
WN

The Gallows

Look down the street!
She is up again
trimmed with a garland
of snow-white bones.

Stiff and haughty
she must be waiting for company
the way she looks around, as if to ask:

"Who is sentenced to visit me today?
Will he debase himself and weep and beg?
Will he be cursing without the words to say what he wants?
Maybe a priest to walk beside him and talk away his fears?
Or a girlfriend? He can fall on his knees crying, I'm innocent!
with all the breath he has left."

But hey, look who's here.
Look at him. Calm and quiet.
Not crying at all, no cursing or yelling.
He has greeted the thing
with clear eyes, asking, "Is this it?"

Now listen to the hush
while the hangman thunders up the steps
and stops in front of the prisoner.
"Is there something you want?"

There is no response
until the thug leans close.

Then the prisoner spits in his face and asks:
"Now do you know?"

The hangman turns white.

ILONA KARMEL
AG

An Army in Retreat

When an army retreats, it is the feet that wear out.
Highways, tracks, the feet of thousands.

Shoulders heavy, through fields, forests and swamps, a
    million, a hundred thousand
Soldiers walk.

Eyes crazed, fear leaps out and blinds them. Hands like rifles,
    obsolete machines,
In the hundreds and the thousands.

Hearts dead on arrival from unutterable terror and pain on
    the road.
(Hearts can be buried and stamped on, stamped down hard.)

But the feet the feet the feet the feet the feet keep going all
    over the world!

HENIA KARMEL
AG

Anniversaries

In my house no mourning candles will ever glisten.
Too many would have to burn—millions.

Then days of anniversaries would follow.
Too many to honor the lost ones, it would take forever.

In my house no mourning candles will ever glisten.
I tell you, there's not even enough time to light them!

My whole life is already a prolonged day of mourning.
Each minute is spent in grief.

What would I do with little teardrop candles
when my heart is like a furnace

that burned up my happiness with the others?

ILONA KARMEL
AG

Memory: Skarzysko

Mud and rags.
Some in crates.
Some sealed in lime
like the spoils of a plague
for carrion.

Deadly effluvia
from the depths of the latrine.
Biers of typhus.

Bad dreams!
What's left of the person
is an appetite
for revenge.

Now obesity
is for lice only.
Humans are emaciated
though one screams
crazily
and one still weeps.

HENIA KARMEL
WN

To the German People

Are you asleep or what?
Blind? Can't hear?
That's the Marseillaise and the crash
of the world falling down.
Hear it? It means freedom
is coming. I bet you want that too.
A red star on Soviet tanks!
Life! Returning while you sleep.
Wake up, people of Germany. Get ready!
Step in time to the Marseillaise.
You better revive your hearts and souls
as if the love of your life was coming home.

Or maybe you don't want freedom.
Just more sleep. Even then
won't you fear the red flag?
If so, wake up!
The workers are on their way.
And on the corner of every German street
a bastille is about to be beaten down
by raised fists. Thank God
her doors will be smashed open.
No more gates!

So hey, who dares go first
into this marvelous chaos?
To hoist the flag on Equality?
And after? When it's over
we will erect a huge structure
out of concrete and steel
and inscribe it—in gold—
with the immortal word
Fraternité!

HENIA KARMEL
WN

At Laban's Grave

Dying isn't always the end.
Sometimes it's the beginning.
It magnifies, for instance,
a single life of action.
It arrives as a shout
from a healthy person.

It is often three:
an overfull heart,
a thought that flies free
and becomes a deed.

It can come as a raised fist,
a manifesto, a summons,
an order (unavoidable)
or suicide to avoid suffering.
All these.

But remember if you ever
walk past this pit in years
to come, someone lived here.
He fought and didn't perish.
No, he didn't die!
With his life he overcame death.

ILONA KARMEL
WN

Meditation in an Air Raid Shelter

For five long years it lay in wait for me.
Its claws were cunning in their reach.
But I slipped away
and a German bullet missed me.
Boxcars from hell didn't bear me to the fire.
My youth and strength overpowered typhus.
Hunger gnawed but didn't rip my guts apart.
I live and look at the world!
My body was never torn to shreds by grenades
and my heart amazingly didn't break
from homesickness.

Years!
After all this, the sound of engines overhead
wouldn't scare me. Steel wings.
Silver wings. Fire belching out of them.
In fact airplanes give me hope again.
Strangely they signal the calm
that comes after the storm.

HENIA KARMEL
WN

My Language

I can't look for a new homeland
Because Poland
Has captivated me with its poetry.
I scratch on a steel plate
My soul in blood, my language.

HENIA KARMEL
AG

Movie

A showing, a show,
in a second-rate theater.
A cheap melodrama
on a cheaper screen.
Time travels by on a gray band.
Or fails unexpectedly.

That's life. A screening
before only two rows
of seats. According to the laws
of motion, shadows
equal time in this machine.
Endless loss and return.

In the real world as well
everything is made of motion.
Images rush past.
They are illusions. Now it is us
dashing forward or standing still
enslaved to a predetermined fate.

That's life. A theater.
A film. Very eerie
when it breaks apart
in a gray evening hour
and the screen turns terribly
and completely white.

HENIA KARMEL
WN

The Converts

Christ pushed us away and Yahweh cursed us.
So now we are homeless.
We want to go back and beg
for forgiveness. But no such luck. We're stuck.

The wind makes us sick
with its empty hiss. Our palms reach into darkness.
No response. Loneliness has a long echo
and a laugh for the converts among us.

We jump at our own utterances.
When you're insane, you can't see anything
up close. You just rush relentlessly
forward. Damned is where you end up.

HENIA KARMEL
WN

The Bastard

Because I was homeless
I was at a loss. Really,
I was an illegitimate child
whose longing howled and like a hound
I scavenged neighborhoods
for a mother's warm touches and breasts.

I wandered a long, long time
and found nothing like a mother
until I found you, Russia.

Russia, hold me,
as if I were your own
against your body
made of golden grain,
your meadows long and yellow
over the Volga river.

Far off the lonely Ackerman steppes
conjure up a great poet
and his sonnets.

I will always love Georgia drenched in sunshine
and its hot starry nights, velvety, intoxicating
and the blue Caucasian sky.
Let me stay.
Let me love
the white Siberian taiga,
brutal as it is,
let me love close up
Odessa and her poets,
the capital of courtesans,
Stalingrad, wet with blood,
and mighty Moscow's steel and cement.

Let me love one place wholeheartedly
and then I will finally forget
that I have no birthright.

HENIA KARMEL
WN

To My Hungarian Brothers

You don't believe what's happening here,
do you, my poor horrified brothers?
You want to know how anyone
could live like this?

I'll tell you.
Hang-dog and helpless as you are
don't be afraid.
Everything here changes and goes away.
Soon you'll learn
how monotonous it all is,
your eyes will lose their curiosity.
You'll stop desiring and the despair
that struggles to grow, will.
Your soul will dull.
So don't let anything move you.
Emotion is unnecessary here.
Dreams bring nothing but grief.

All you need here are a pair of strong legs
to drag you through the gray days
and patience.

HENIA KARMEL
WN

No One Is Calling

"Let's ride on. No one is calling."
Adam Mickiewicz

Nothing changes, every day it's the same.

An unresponsive street, the prison gate.

Sometimes a dream stupidly hangs on

And searches for a smile in a cold face.

Sometimes I stop and hallucinate

And hear a voice calling my name.

Malevolent silence is all I get then

And so I move on, dragging my feet
With a "Come on. Let's walk. No one is calling."

HENIA KARMEL
WN

And My Songs

Now my songs will always be about the suffering
That only brothers and sisters could understand,
About days when we were deluded
—No, afflicted!—by hope for the future.

From now on my work will only find a home
In those, like me, who knew sheer terror
And faced both the end and an unknown.
Those two points that point down.

Now I can only write for people
Who, like me, learned how to wait
In a state of exhaustion and starvation,
Who lay down with the despair of separation!

Now I can only sing from experience
To others who lived inside barbed wire.
And to those armies of people I send one sound
In the form of a song. Let it be as pure as tears.

HENIA KARMEL
AG

To Jews Abroad

(To Mr. Sternbuch)

When Rabbi Kook came back
from his vacation he sent out
a proclamation:
"Everyone! Fast
on behalf of European Jews!"

At once the secretary
and chief of JOINT
pulled out the register:
Give this to the Rear
and this to the Front
and this to prisoners for sausages.

Mr. Sternbuch of St. Gall
kept track of the markets
because he always sent raisins
to the Polish Jews on Easter.
Chairman Weizmann in Palestine
was nervous.
What would they say in London?
What should he do with this rabble?

Sir, calm down or the heat
will kill you. Smooth
your thick brow. The rabble
will be dead long before that.

Meantime, thanks, brothers
for the jams and sardines
and for your fasting
for sausages and raisins.

Thanks, thanks. If God grants
that I don't die,
then I'll throw all of these treats
back into your faces!
and run as fast as I can—thanks but no thanks—
away from Palestine.

HENIA KARMEL
WN

My Freedom

When freedom came, it was strange:
chilly, blurred, unrecognizable.
I was so surprised
I could only stare straight into space.
My heart still beat
but when I shut my eyes, I felt sick.
Unable to face my freedom.

It wasn't what it used to be
but morbidly turned around.
Ghosts grasped the white edges
of my hospital linens
and shook and wouldn't let go
like a pack of maniacs making me
afraid to look liberty in the face.

It had come a few days too late.
I had already lost everything
that can never be returned.
Even happiness had died with the rest
inside an isolated hospital ward.
Freedom? I can't face it!

HENIA KARMEL
WN

Letter from the Hospital

In the hospital only the hospital is left.
A white rectangle.
A bed and ceiling.
A window's blue flowering
in a hieroglyphic weave
of branches. That's it.
On the next planet
a sort of man wheezes.
Lung-gasps, larynx-spit.
His hand waves away
the world that keeps
returning. His heart
won't stop its feverish pump.
He jumps up, his bandages drop.
On his face, blood.
He shouts, he suffers.

I know it's you he wants, Sister Gentle.
Please come.
His eyes are calling for you
not to be afraid of him.
Your footsteps in the corridor
bring such happiness.
That's all there is here.
You and waiting for you.
Will you come to me when I give up hope?
When hospital white drives me mad?
You will. That's the only good
I know of and believe.
Oh and the window
will be blue with spring.

ILONA KARMEL
WN

Second Letter

It is winter.
What more is there to say?
It is what it was when we were still alive.
And where did you disappear to?
And your eyes that I loved?

I keep looking at you
to calm myself down—
at your photograph, that is—it once made me cry.
I, un-alive, am writing to you who went away.

Yes. It is winter.
The frost is as strong as alcohol.
If I could just get drunk on it!
But then why bother? I'm drunk
on sorrow, and as low as the dusk.

I wonder if you remember
snow-covered fields
and mountains swirling under clouds,
how the earth becomes indistinguishable
from the sky.

The borders disappear as before.
The earth is as it was
when we were still alive.
Why did we believe, stupidly, that the sun
would shut off and the world stop
when we were out of it?

No, it is as it was.
Dawn, dusk, etcetera, people who laugh
and cry, bless, curse, don't notice you left.
And I do the same, almost.

I'm writing this on a frosty day.
Halfway to you. The world slips through
the window as human voices
long beyond the range of my thoughts.
That snow and earth-line, very far away.

HENIA KARMEL
WN

Purim 1946

A hunchbacked candle
and its weeping wax.
A cantor with shaky hands
and the scroll he holds.
Yellow and old . . .

Is it memory that makes him call
for retaliation?

Because I don't understand how
he and the scroll survived
when the years eliminated most of us.

And his weak voice?

I don't understand
how he can sing such a song
and people join in. He bends
and trembles over the yellow thing.

Everything seems the same
as when the holidays
meant fragrant cake and almonds
and people knew how to rejoice.

Everything seems the same
as then, but now weighted down
with a terrible grief.
Vengeance is not sweet.

Behind the candle
and the scroll
and the cantor and his shouts
for revenge

what do I see deep
in the darkest areas of the place?
The prayerful gaze of my father
and his hands that blessed—stretched out—

HENIA KARMEL
AG

Autobiography

Youth

Hush. Close your mouth.
Raise your hand
into a clenched fist.
This is youth.
Another story altogether.
Bitter and sad.
Hard and unavoidable.

These memories won't quit.
They even hurt.
It was the autumn of '39.
How to describe (in what language?
fire?) that time.
When she arrived, she, youth,
she, without romance,
or poetic introductions.
Distant reader, she came
with thunder, soldiers,
cannons, machine guns.

Youth. No more fables.
I see the dark ditch and us in it.
Overhead, horrible wings.
Shock, screams, smoke, sun
and a shaking ground.

What was The World to us
crashed down. Gray petals
of smoke unfurled
into a red conflagration.

From that moment on,
it would always be the same.
A mother's terror
and still her comforting hands.

Both of these, and that avalanche.

Time staggered forward
without mercy
carrying each person with him.
I grew from fifteen to sixteen.

The days were voracious,
like creatures that clawed
at whatever we took with us.
The closest, the most loved.

They clawed until they dug
a horrible void into
our childish faces!
We grew old, dull-eyed, dry.

Only hate stayed strong.
Little, but quite sufficient
to get us through the graveyard days
and give us more bitter knowledge.

The art of the closed fist
the clever closed fist.

Don't scream from pain.
Don't express rage.

Cut from your lexicon
the words *happiness, laughter,*
and change *love* to *hate.*
Cut all words that would be a waste.

The simple and difficult art
of self-censorship is to ensure
that no heart exists.

Mother's hands, once capable
only of arranging flowers in a vase,
were now hard, she learned
how to deflect a blow with them.

Love made them tough
while her face grew yellow,
her eyes lost their life,
until her heart gave up the struggle.

So friend, that is all
I can remember. You count.
How many graves? How many days?
It is now 1945.

Blood, a taste of morphine,
bad dreams, no more mother's hands . . .

This is the epilogue, friend.
From my life inside four walls.

I have no childhood dreams, only
visitations from the fearful
nightmares of those years.

Worse for being known
but now with nowhere to run
for comfort from them.
No maternal hands.

The story ends here
when I am twenty.

ILONA KARMEL

AG

An Open Letter to Julian Tuwim—1947

Dear Sir:

I am taking the liberty of sending you some of my poems—for one reason. Because you, like me, stood at the gates of the temple in which it was "forbidden to pray." Because you, like me, felt "the great reserves of spirit, accumulated for nothing," because you, too, heard the "song of the damned."

Maybe you'll find these poems too simple, commonplace, not worthy of notice. Maybe you'll even throw them away without reading them all the way through. But please remember one thing—these poems are real, not just scribblings. They come from behind the wires of a concentration camp. There was simply no time in that place for scribbling.

These poems came about when I was still creating myself, experiencing the pain of separation. For the first time I heard the words *not allowed.* I then came to know the meaning of the word *never.* I came to know longing, homesickness, and my first human tears. (I don't want to bore you.) At that point these were not yet poems, but a presentiment of them in my heart, complaining and weeping, but I didn't yet know the magic of words enough to express them.

But then, weeks and months passed without a pen to write with. Well, not completely. I could write with whitened lips and trembling fingers on countless forms, pieces of blank paper, blue, white, and yellow paper. Each of these innocent pastel-colored cards, my dear sir, each one conjured deportation, selection. Let's not mince words: each one had the breath of death.

So began those horrible days when I ran like a hunted animal from town to town, from village to village, anywhere to get away from Them. But They caught up with us. And every little piece of paper was a little shred of living matter torn from me—father, friend, home.

A person now no longer a person, no longer creating herself, is tied to life by a thousand flimsy threads. Each day one of these threads breaks: the tip whirls off into the abyss. Ever more alone. Yes, those were terrifying days.

It was then I learned what savage fear was like, the longing, not for something distant or remote, but for what is lost forever, something that can never return.

Never was the word that burned in my brain ever more powerfully, ever more grimly. That's when I learned the whistles of bullets, the crack of gunfire, the ominous pounding of feet, the agony of waiting. ("They're here! Over there! Here! They killed . . . They caught!") Then I got to know the cry "God, I'll never make it." I became familiar with frightening places—prisons, torture chambers, and places where others perished, the dearest ones, where the walls cried out, "Do not forget me or this wrong!"

This lasted with variations for weeks, months and years. Perhaps you wonder if I am exaggerating? How I could have survived, you may ask? If so, sir, you know nothing of life. It lasted, that's all. The walls of the ghetto turned into the barbed wires of the camp. As a person matures, she constantly learns something new.

So there was pain, common physical pain, when your face gets slashed by a whip, blood dripping down in narrow trickles like tears. I didn't know what tears meant then.

A person learned then that death could come—and oh so easily—without a pastel-colored courtesy card. It lies day and night, around every corner, behind every wall, whistling, inimical.

We got to know the creaky song of the gallows. We saw a

bloody body dangling in the air, just because she was young and sang about Katiusha. I'm not exaggerating here.

We came to know that fear can do anything to a human being.

We came to know what hunger and slave labor were.

The threads linking the point to life kept on snapping and disappearing faster and deeper.

But then the poems appeared. They came because they had to, because a person had to have a sanctuary, where no one could brutally intrude, so as not to be completely alone.

You will surmise that one didn't write in comfort, at a desk. We wrote them in the interminable nights, on a sweltering bed of planks, almost unconsciously, in a fever.

These are those poems.

And this is why they are so strange, disordered, chaotic, and deranged with fright. This is why they are so uniform in content, as monotonous as the monotonous gray and hopeless prison days.

This is why they resonate with the selfsame rhythm. They were dictated by the din of bullets, the crack of gunshots, the growling of machine guns.

In the end this is why they are so poor in words, deprived of beautiful phrases. This is an ordinary, primal cry, the rattle of one being choked.

I don't ask you, sir, for a gentle appreciation. On the contrary, please be ruthless and honest. Do not be driven by courtesy. These poems were never written with popularity or fame in mind. They are only SONGS OF THE DAMNED.

HENIA KARMEL

AG

On vacation outside Kraków, Henia with her arm on Ilona's shoulder; photograph taken by their father, 1937.

Ilona kissing Henia, 1938.

Ilona and Henia inside the Karolinska Institute in Stockholm, where Ilona was recovering from her injuries, 1946.

Ilona (in wheelchair) and Henia (hiding her pregnant belly) in the garden of the Karolinska Institute, Stockholm, 1946.

Henia and Leon, 1945.

Afterword

I wish to express my personal thanks and gratitude, as well as the gratitude of my family members, for what Fanny Howe has done to memorialize the Karmel sisters. When I first read her translations, I made a very complimentary statement—that the essence she conveyed was truer than the original poems. Having spent most of my life in America, I now feel much more comfortable with American English than I do with Polish. I consider myself part of the English-speaking world, and I am proud that these poems are now available to that world.

The Hebrew word *haskama* refers to permission given by noted rabbis for the publication of a Hebrew book. Historically, the main reason for issuing these permits *(haskamot)* was to prevent publication of a work that was likely to create ill will on the part of the readership. This self-imposed censorship was first introduced at the rabbinical conference at Ferrara, Italy, in 1554, one year after the public burning of the Talmud. It eventually became the forerunner of what we consider nowadays to be copyright. Similarly, the word *imprimatur* refers to a license to print or publish. Either word applies in this case. I give my fullest permission for these translations to be published. It is a voluntary expression of my deep gratitude, appreciation, and goodwill.

Leon Wolfe

Notes on the Translations

FANNY HOWE

It is important that readers understand the process of translation that took place with these poems. First of all, I want to say that the intention behind this collection has been to make *poetry* out of poetry, not to provide an exact rendering of the original Polish. This does not mean that I left the originals behind; far from it. It means that I adapted the literal translations that I was given by the two translators, turning them into forms of contemporary poetry. The two sisters were not creating documents for scholars to use in studying the effects of forced labor. They wanted to make poems.

That is why this was my single goal: to come to the poetry as a poet . . . that is, to continue the aspiration of Ilona and Henia Karmel, who were writing under intolerable conditions. I took up the task because of my long friendship with Ilona, who was now gone, and because I wanted to make a contribution to the poetry of resistance as it continues through history to this very hour. Enslavement, imprisonment, torture: here they are again.

Why did these girls work on poems in the middle of hell? It

organized their experience? It gave them vent for their outrage? It helped them hold on to their childhood through a memory that only language can revive? Out of obedience to some biolinguistic drive in the human brain? Why do so many prisoners write poetry? I hope that a Polish reader will someday study the originals as explicit evidence (revealed in structure and word choice) of a state of mind that is wrought by oppression everywhere. But Henia's concluding letter to Julian Tuwim tells us a great deal.

Because I am not a Polish reader, I could only come to these questions secondhand, and then by immersing myself in these poems as stand-ins for experience. In this sense, it was a labor of imagination. I know how writing notes during an experience, then scribbling and correcting them, like one chasing a hidden form inside a chaotic thicket, rests the mind; it is a yogic discipline. Therefore I can imagine Ilona's and Henia's fierce postures, bent over paper in a hard darkness at night, and I can at least sense what it meant to them. The search for music, beat, clarity . . . meaning.

I did not add anything new to any one of the poems given to me in English translation. But I did take away words and phrases that were repeated or seemed unnecessarily prolonged or undeveloped (for poetry) because of the hurried conditions under which they were written. For the most part I chose to work on poems that formed complete thoughts and trajectories and juggled extraordinary images.

I avoided most poems that used high and archaic language, although I understood that these were attempts at salvaging something of the old culture that once kept the girls safe at school and at home. Instead I focused (as did the translators) on the poems that emerged from the ordeal in a direct way. Each translator gave me a small batch of poems to work on. I carried them around with me for many weeks, sometimes months, and treated them the way I treat first drafts of my own work.

I scratched and erased, and tried again another word or shape, over and over, until I found the phantom that was rooted inside the words and was ready to walk. I moved some words from one place to another for the sake of sound, because for me each line in a poem is a sound unit. If the sound of a word had a more secure ring beside another word than where it was in the original and moving it did not interfere with meanings, I moved it . . . Afterwards I showed my finished piece to the translator to make sure I had done no damage, and he responded with criticism or agreement. All these translations have had several readings by Polish speakers.

The original Polish poems are not complicated, or very metaphorical, or experimental; they are straightforward in vocabulary and message. Many are awkward and unpolished, which is not surprising given the conditions under which they were written. At least this is what I was told by several Polish readers. Again, Henia's letter to Julian Tuwim says it all.

The translators chose the poems they felt had the greatest potential or were closest to being complete and resonant. Almost always these were poems dealing very directly with life in the camps and Henia's and Ilona's response to that. The difficulty for me was not about interpretation but about reincarnation. Could I bring these poems back to life in a new body and a new world?

It turned out that the best way to do that was through cutting. And this fact, more than any other, reminded me of the great obligation of translation: to seek the impersonal. The impersonal is the one thing unburdened by attributes, the free one, the one everyone knows in all worlds, the one capable of heroism.

I realize that these are only the first English versions of the originals; there may be many more in time. There are more writings by the sisters that remain unpublished, many of them in English. For the interest of the reader, below I give two of the *most extreme* examples of my editing, so the reader can look at my translation and have an idea of what was involved. Here is an English rendering given to me by Arie Galles:

> All around did stare with a kind of fear
> Whispering something, horribly hurrying
> And the rag on the stretchers was expiring . . .
> And at the end, four, as in nightmares
> Carried on shoulders bent low
> A human bundle, hanging inertly
> And they could not cope
> The bundle weighed down horribly to the ground
> The bundle bled and screamed incoherently.

I pared away the excess of participles and dangling clauses in order to bring forward the grotesque fact at the center of the poem: a human had become an "it." Here is my version of the last stanza of "Procession":

> The parade went on
> while we watched in dread.
> The rag man on the litter was dying.
> And at the end, four from a nightmare
> lugged on their heavy shoulders
> a bundled body.

They couldn't cope and let it drop.
It screamed in its own blood.

In another case of pruning back, I received this literal English
rendering by Warren Niesłuchowski from Henia's "The Bastard":

Russia, let me fall in love with your pale, broad meadows,
Golden with grain, the grainfields on the Volga
The distant and doleful Ackerman steppes
(Those which the soul of the great poet
Conjured in the immortal and wistful sonnets).

And let me love [that] Georgia drenched in sunlight
Her bright nights, torrid and hot
The intoxicating Aksam[?] nights
And [that] most blue Caucasian sky
And even the white Siberian taiga, which [all] haunt us with
    [their] bloody past
Let me, let me fall in love [*po-kochac* = 'en-amor'] with
    grand, great love [*milosc*].

And let me love Odessa of the poets, the capital of
    courtesans
And the streets of Stalingrad drenched in blood
And the mighty Moscow of steel-cement
Let me [fall in] love to the death.

For only then will I forget
My great and ancient wrong
And that I am—a bastard.

Again, I felt that this version of the poem was overburdened
with dangling clauses and excess adjectives; I cut it down to the

most essential images in order to bring forward the shape and drive of the erotic longing for a homeland, in this case Russia:

Russia, hold me,
as if I were your own
against your body
made of golden grain,
your meadows long and yellow
over the Volga river.

Far off the lonely Ackerman steppes
conjure up a great poet
and his sonnets.

I will always love Georgia drenched in sunshine
and its hot starry nights, velvety, intoxicating
and the blue Caucasian sky.
Let me stay.
Let me love
the white Siberian taiga,
brutal as it is,
let me love close up
Odessa and her poets,
the capital of courtesans,
Stalingrad, wet with blood,
and mighty Moscow's steel and cement.

Let me love one place wholeheartedly
and then I will finally forget
that I have no birthright.

One final note: I tried to avoid using the word *death* in my adaptations. Instead I hoped to conjure up other names for it because all language stops and goes to ground before that one word. And under the circumstances in which these poems were written, that word, when it was not quite fulfilled, took form as incarceration, wires, hunger, guns, gallows, factories, and then, when uttered, the word itself meant nothing.

To prove this to myself, in 2004 I visited Buchenwald during the last week of January. The black trees were like a preformation of words. Black shadows, black and cryptic twists that were a literature grown from the surrounding silence. Black twigs, snow, the light across the field that wanted to sing. This was the end of language.

About the Translators

Arie A. Galles (AG) was born in Tashkent, Uzbekistan. He grew up in Poland and Israel, coming to the United States in 1958. He received his BFA in 1968 from the Tyler School of Fine Arts of Temple University and his MFA in 1971 from the University of Wisconsin. Galles taught at Fairleigh Dickinson University for many years and is now at Soka University in Southern California. His paintings, based on aerial views, have been exhibited nationally, including at multiple solo shows at the O. K. Harris Gallery in New York and the Zolla/Liberman Gallery in Chicago. His works are in public and private collections in the United States and abroad.

Warren Niesłuchowski (WN) was born in a Polish refugee camp in Germany after the Second World War and was raised in Massachusetts. During the American war in Vietnam he lived in France and performed with the Bread and Puppet Theatre throughout Europe and Iran and then in a Parisian theatrical collective pursuing the methods of Polish director Jerzy Grotowski's

Teatr-Laboratorium. For the past dozen years, after studies in linguistics and social theory at Harvard University, he has been working with and for artists, first at P. S. 1 Contemporary Art Center in New York and then independently, as a writer, speaker, translator, editor, and collaborator.

Bibliography

Henia Karmel-Wolfe
  The Baders of Jacob Street, 1971
  Marek and Lisa, 1984

Ilona Karmel
  Stephania, 1953
  An Estate of Memory, 1969

Henryka and Ilona Karmel
  Spiew Za Drutami (Song behind barbed wire), 1947

Acknowledgments of Permissions

All works by Henia Karmel and all photographs appear courtesy of the estate of Henia Karmel-Wolfe.

All works by Ilona Karmel appear courtesy of the estate of Ilona Karmel.

Leon Wolfe's afterword appears courtesy of the author.

Translations from the Polish by Arie A. Galles appear courtesy of the translator.

Translations from the Polish by Warren Niesłuchowski appear courtesy of the translator.

Designer	Claudia Smelser
Text and display	Bulmer
Compositor	BookMatters, Berkeley
Printer and binder	Friesens Corporation